Mark Twain Presents The Adventures of Tom Sawyer
Copyright © 2013
Mike Parker

Published by WordCrafts Theatrical Press
912 E. Lincoln St.
Tullahoma, TN 37388
www.wordcrafts.net

MARK TWAIN PRESENTS

THE ADVENTURES OF TOM SAWYER

adapted for the stage
by
Mike Parker

Playwright's Notes

Mark Twain Presents The Adventures of Tom Sawyer

Tom Sawyer, perhaps even more than Peter Pan, represents the quintessential spirit of boyhood. Tom, Huck, Becky, Aunt Polly, Sid and even Injun Joe are archetypal characters that resonate deeply in the American psyche. (It should be here noted that "Injun Joe" is a name, not a pejorative, in much the same as vein as "Tex" Ritter, "Wild" Bill Hickok or the Washington "Redskins." It is the name assigned to the character by Mark Twain, and I have elected to maintain it as is.)

While it is entirely possible to produce this play using sumptuous sets, it is not necessary to do so. I've attempted to write the play so that it can be produced on a variety of stages by theatres with either large or small budgets. The original production by Middle Tennessee's Lamplighter's Theatre Company, used an innovated set designed by resident director, Nathan Owen, that employed nothing beyond plywood boxes of different sizes that could be rearranged in moments to create the different scenes.

I believe it is the responsibility of the playwright to write the play, and that it is the responsibility of the director to direct. As such, I have refrained from inserting many stage directions, leaving the director free to direct the show as he or she sees fit.

Cheers,

Mike Parker

<u>Characters</u>
In Order of Appearance

Huckleberry Finn
Mark Twain
Aunt Polly
Tom Sawyer
Sid Sawyer
Ben Rogers
Amy Lawrence
Joe Harper
Mary Sawyer
Mr. Walters
Judge Thatcher
Mrs. Thatcher
Becky Thatcher
Muff Potter
Injun Joe
Dr. Robinson
Jeff Thatcher
Prosecutor
Mrs. Sereny Harper
Pard
Widow Douglas

ACT I

SETTING: An empty stage.

AT RISE: Actors in costume begin setting the stage with AUNT POLLY'S home. All except AUNT POLLY exit once the stage is set. HUCKLEBERRY FINN notices the audience and steps forward to address them. MARK TWAIN enters while HUCK is talking.

HUCK
Evenin'. My name is Huckleberry Finn. You don't know about me without you have read a book by the name of *The Adventures of Tom Sawyer*. That book was made by Mr. Mark Twain, and he told the truth, mainly, although was some things which he stretched. Shoot, I ain't never seen nobody but lied one time or 'nother - without it was Aint Polly, or the Widder, or maybe Mary. Aint Polly, Tom's Aint Polly that is, and Mary, and the Widder Douglas is all told about in that book, which is mostly a true book, with some stretchers thrown in, as I said before.

Now the way that book winds up is this: Tom and me found the money that the robbers hid in the cave, and it made us rich...

MARK TWAIN
Huckleberry. Don't you have something that needs attending to?

HUCK
Oh, uh, yessir, Mr. Twain. I was just telling the folks how most

of the time you told the truth and...
>   (Returns to help set the stage.)

MARK TWAIN

As my young friend said, *most* of the adventures recorded in this play really occurred; one or two were experiences of my own, the rest those of boys who were schoolmates of mine. Huck Finn is drawn from life; Tom Sawyer also, but not from an individual. He is a combination of the characteristics of three boys whom I knew, and therefore belongs to the composite order of architecture.

The odd superstitions touched upon in this story were all prevalent among children in the West during the period of this story - that is to say, one hundred and sixty or seventy years ago.

Although this play is intended mainly for the entertainment of boys and girls, I hope it will not be shunned by men and women on that account, for part of my plan has been to try to pleasantly remind adults of what they once were themselves; of how they felt and thought and talked, and what strange enterprises they sometimes engaged in.
>   (TWAIN exits.)

AUNT POLLY

Tom? Tom! What's gone with that boy? You Tom! Well, I lay if I get hold of you I'll...I never did see the beat of that boy. Y-o-u-u Tom!

>   (TOM tries to sneak out of the closet. AUNT
>   POLLY hears him and grabs him by the back of
>   his overalls.)

AUNT POLLY

There! I mighta thought of looking in that closet. What you been doing in there?

TOM
Nothing.

AUNT POLLY
Nothing! Look at your hands. And look at your mouth. You been in the jam again. Forty times I've said if you didn't let that jam alone I'd skin you alive. Hand me that switch.

TOM
Look out, behind you!

> (AUNT POLLY whirls around. TOM flees out the back door. AUNT POLLY stands surprised for a moment, and then breaks into a gentle laugh.)

AUNT POLLY
Hang the boy, cain't I never learn anything? Ain't he played tricks enough like that for me to be looking out for him by this time? But old fools is the biggest fools they is. Cain't learn an old dog new tricks, as the saying goes. He 'pears to know just how long he can torment me before I get my dander up, and he knows if he can put me off for a minute or make me laugh, it's all down again and I cain't hit him a lick.

I ain't doing my duty by that boy, and that's the Lord's own truth. *Spare the rod and spile the child*, as the Good Book says. I'm a laying up sin and suffering for the both of us, I know, but laws-a-me! he's my own dead sister's boy, poor thing, and I ain't got the heart to lash him. Every time I let him off, my conscience does hurt me so, and every time I hit him my old heart 'most breaks.

Well-a-well, *man that is born of woman is of few days and full of trouble*, as the Good Book says, and I reckon it's so. He'll play hooky this evening, and I'll be obleeged to make him work on Saturday when all the other boys is having holiday. He hates work more than he hates anything else. But I've got to do some of my duty or I'll be the ruination of the child.

> (Fade to black. When the lights rise TOM appears with a bucket of whitewash and a long-handled brush. He begins a half hearted attempt at painting. SID comes along, toting a tin pail, and singing Buffalo Gals.)

TOM
Say, Sid, I'll fetch the water for you, if you'll whitewash some.

SID
Cain't, Tom. Aint Polly is paying me two whole bits to fetch this water. She told me I got to go along with myself and get this water and not stop to fool around with nobody. She says she 'specs Tom is going to ask me to whitewash, and she told me go 'long with myself and tend to my own business, and let Tom tend to the whitewashin'.

TOM
Oh, never you mind what Aint Polly said, Sid. That's the way she always talks. Gimme the bucket. I won't be gone only a minute. She won't ever know.

SID
Oh, I daren't, Tom. Aint Polly, she 'lowed she'd take and tear the head off'n me, if I let you talk me into doing your work for you. 'Deed she would, too.

TOM
She never licks anybody. Whacks 'em over the head with her thimble, that's all, and who cares for that. She talks awful, but

talk don't hurt. I'll give you a white alley, Sid. And besides, I'll show you my sore toe!

> (SID puts down his pail, takes the white alley (a marble), and bends over the toe while TOM unwinds the bandage. AUNT POLLY approaches, paddle in hand, and delivers a quick swat to both rear ends. The next moment SID is flying down the street with his pail and TOM is whitewashing with vigor. AUNT POLLY retires back into the house. BEN ROGERS enters in high spirits, munching on an apple, ready to poke fun at TOM for having to work on Saturday. TOM pays him no mind.)

BEN
Hello, Tom. You got to work, hey? Say, I'm fixin' to go swimming. Don't you wish you could? But of course you'd druther work, wouldn't you? 'Course you would!

TOM
Why, it's you, Ben. I warn't noticing.

BEN
Too busy working, I reckon.

TOM
What do you call work?

BEN
Why, ain't that work?

TOM
Well, maybe it is and maybe it ain't. All I know is, it suits Tom Sawyer.

BEN

Oh come, now. You don't mean to let on that you like it?

TOM

Like it? Well, I don't see why I oughtn't to like it. Does a boy get a chance to whitewash a fence every day?

> (BEN stops nibbling his apple. TOM continues to paint, steps back to note the effect, and adds a touch here and there. BEN watches every move, getting more and more interested.)

BEN

Say, Tom, let me whitewash a little.

TOM

No, I reckon it wouldn't hardly do, Ben. You see, Aint Polly's awful particular about this fence, it being right here on the street and all. 'Course if it was the back fence I wouldn't mind and she wouldn't. Yes, she's awful particular about this fence; it's got to be done real careful; I reckon there ain't one boy in a thousand, maybe two thousand, that can do it the way it's got to be done.

BEN

No, is that so? Oh come on, lemme just try. I'd let you, if you was me, Tom.

TOM

Ben, I'd like to, honest; but well, Sid wanted to do it, and she wouldn't let Sid. Now don't you see what kind of fix I'm in? If you was to tackle this fence and anything was to happen to it...

BEN

Oh, shucks, I'll be careful. Lemme try. Say, I'll give you the core of my apple.

TOM
Well, here… No, Ben, now don't. I'm afeard…

BEN
I'll give you all of it!

> (TOM gives up the brush with reluctance in his face. Several more boys enter, encounter TOM, and are relieved of their valuables for a chance to whitewash the fence. During this time MARK TWAIN enters and begins his discourse.)

MARK TWAIN
Tom had a nice, good, idle time, with plenty of company - and the fence ended up with three coats of whitewash on it. If he hadn't run out of whitewash he would have bankrupted every boy in the village.

Without knowing it, Tom had discovered a great law of human action, namely, that in order to make a man, or a boy, covet a thing, it is only necessary to make the thing difficult to attain. If he had been a great and wise philosopher, like the writer of this play, he would have comprehended that *Work* consists of whatever a body is obliged to do, and that *Play* consists of whatever a body is not obliged to do.

The boy mused awhile over the substantial change which had taken place in his worldly circumstances, and then wended his way toward headquarters to report.

> (During TWAIN'S discourse all the boys drift away until only TOM is left. TOM walks inside the house to find AUNT POLLY.)

TOM
Mayn't I go and play now, Aint Polly?

AUNT POLLY
What, a'ready? How much have you done?

TOM
It's all done.

AUNT POLLY
Tom, don't lie to me. I can't bear it.

TOM
I ain't lying, Aint Polly; it is all done.

(AUNT POLLY goes to see for herself. TOM
follows her out.)

AUNT POLLY
Well, I never. There's no getting round it, you can work when
you've a mind to. But it's powerful seldom you've a mind to,
I'm bound to say. Well, go 'long and play; but mind you get
back some time this week, or I'll tan you.

(TOM exits as the lights dim. Spot on MARK
TWAIN.)

MARK TWAIN
The sun rose Sunday morning upon a tranquil world, and
beamed down upon the peaceful village like a benediction.
Breakfast over, Aunt Polly had family worship: it began with a
prayer built from the ground up of solid courses of Scriptural
quotations, welded together with a thin mortar of originality; and
as if from the summit of Sinai she delivered a grim chapter of the
Mosaic Law.

Then Tom girded up his loins to "get his verses." Sid had already
learned his. Tom bent all his energies to the memorizing of five
verses, and he chose a part of the Sermon on the Mount, because

he could find no verses that were... shorter.

> (Lights rise on AUNT POLLY'S home. TWAIN
> exits. MARY, SID, TOM, and AUNT POLLY
> are inside.)

TOM
Blessed are the...a...a...

MARY
Poor.

TOM
Yes! Poor; blessed are the poor...a...a...

MARY
In spirit.

TOM
In spirit; blessed are the poor in spirit, for they...they...

MARY
Theirs.

TOM
For theirs. Blessed are the poor in spirit, for theirs is the kingdom
of heaven. Blessed are they that mourn, for they...they...

MARY
Sh—

TOM
Don't 'shush' me!

MARY
Shall.

TOM

Oh...shall! For they shall...for they shall...mourn. Blessed are they that shall...they that...uh...they that shall mourn, for they shall...shall what?

Why don't you tell me, Mary? What do you want to be so mean for?

MARY

Oh, Tom, I'm not teasing you. I wouldn't do that. You must go and learn it again. Don't you be discouraged, Tom. You'll manage it. And if you do, I'll give you something ever so nice.

TOM

What is it, Mary? Tell me what it is.

MARY

Never you mind, Tom. You know if I say it's nice, it is nice.

TOM

You bet you that's so, Mary. All right, I'll tackle it again.
            (Lights dim as TOM continues to practice his
            verses. Lights come back up as TOM recites his
            verse to MARY.)
Blessed are they that mourn, for they shall be comforted.

MARY

Now aren't you proud, Tom? Aren't you just a fine scholar? In Sunday School they'll give you a blue ticket for reciting that verse. But because you've worked so hard, I've got something ever so nice for you. I ordered it by mail, all the way for St. Louie.
            (MARY hands TOM a small package.)

TOM

All the way from St. Louie?

MARY

It cost me twelve and a half cents. Well, aren't you going to open it?

TOM

> (TOM opens the package and takes out a jackknife.)

It's a Barlow knife! A sure-'nough Barlow knife! Wait'll I show this to Ben Rogers. Won't he just be green. Thank you, Mary!

> (TOM gives MARY a quick hug and then runs out the door shouting about his sure-'nough Barlow knife.)

MARY

Sid. Come along now. We'll be late for Sunday School.

> (SID, MARY, and AUNT POLLY exit the house on their way to church. As they leave some cast members remove the home while others set up the Sunday School room. MARK TWAIN takes center stage.)

MARK TWAIN

In Tom Sawyer's day, few children had a Bible to call their own, a situation certain denominations attempted to rectify by the use of what you might today call 'positive reinforcement.' As each child came to recite their lessons, they were rewarded with a small ticket. A blue ticket was pay for reciting two verses. Ten blue tickets equaled a red one, ten red tickets equaled a yellow one. For ten yellow tickets the superintendent gave the child a very plainly bound Bible, worth forty cents in those times.

How many of you would have the industry and application to memorize two thousand verses? And yet Mary had acquired two Bibles in this way - it was the patient work of two years.

Only the older pupils managed to keep their tickets and stick to their tedious work long enough to get a Bible, and so the delivery of such a prize was a rare and noteworthy circumstance. It is likely that Tom's spiritual stomach had never truly hungered for one of those prizes, but unquestionably his entire being longed for the glory that came with it.

TOM
Say, Ben, got a yaller ticket?

BEN
Yes.

TOM
What'll you take for her?

BEN
What'll you give?

TOM
Piece of lickrish and a fish-hook.

BEN
Less see 'em.

> (JUDGE THATCHER enters along with MRS. THATCHER and their daughter, BECKY. TOM is instantly smitten.)

TOM
Who is that?

JOE
That's Jeff Thatcher's brother. My Ma said he's the County Judge, all the way from Constantinople, pert near twelve miles away. My Ma said he's traveled all over the world.

AMY

I hear the county court-house has a real tin roof.

BEN

I hear Constantinople has a real, paved street.

SID

I hear in Constantinople some folks got their outhouse right inside their home.

(All the others look at SID as if he is insane.)

SID

Well, that's what I hear. Aint Polly said they call it a Water Closet. That's what she said.

JOE

That's Judge Thatcher's daughter up there with him. My Ma said her name's Becky, Becky Thatcher, and my Ma said she was the smartest and best behaved little girl she had ever seen.

AMY

Well, ain't she just sumpthin'.

TOM

I think she's beautiful.

AMY

What?!

TOM

I didn't say nuthin'.

MR. WALTERS

Now, children, I want you all to sit up just as straight and pretty as you can and give me all your attention. My, how good it makes me feel to see so many bright, clean little faces assembled in a place like this, learning to do right and be good. We have some very special guests with us today, and our own lawyer, Mr. Jeff Thatcher, is going to introduce them to you.

(Polite applause as JEFF THATCHER walks to the front, and shakes hands with JUDGE THATCHER.)

BEN
Look at him, Joe! He's a'going up there. He's a'going to shake hands with him. He *is* shaking hands with him! By jings, don't you wish you was Jeff?

JEFF
Good morning, children. This is my brother, the Honorable Judge Horace Thatcher, and his lovely wife, Mrs. Sophie Thatcher. They will be staying with me for a few months before departing our shores for England, where Judge Thatcher will be serving our great country as special envoy to the Court of St. James in London! While they are here, their daughter, Becky will be our guest. I want you all to make her feel right at home.

MR. WALTERS
Judge Thatcher has graciously consented to present a Bible to any child who may have earned one. Wouldn't that be a marvelous experience?
(He looks over the class, hoping someone has the tickets for a Bible.)
Isn't there anyone who has earned a Bible? Count your tickets, please. Anyone?

(There is dead silence as TOM scoots out of his seat and makes his way to the front. MR. WALTERS is stunned, and embarrassed.)

MR. WALTERS
Is there something I can do for you, Thomas?

TOM
I come to claim my Bible, Mr. Walters.

MR. WALTERS
This is no time for foolishness, Thomas. Judge Thatcher is a great personage and…

TOM
I ain't funnin' you, Mr. Walters. I got the tickets.

>   (TOM holds out his tickets and MR. WALTERS counts them out. He is incredulous.)

MR. WALTERS
Nine yellow tickets, nine red tickets and ten blue ones. Well, in all my born days. I never. Well, then. Well, uh, Judge Thatcher, this young man has, apparently, memorized two thousand verses, and is entitled to a Bible. Sir, would you do the honors?

JUDGE THATCHER
The honor would be mine. You are obviously a fine, studious little man. Now, what is your name?

TOM
Tom.

JUDGE THATCHER
Just Tom? Surely there is more to it than that.

MR. WALTERS
Speak up, Thomas. And tell the gentleman your other name. And say 'sir.' You mustn't forget your manners.

TOM
Thomas. Thomas Sawyer...sir.

JUDGE THATCHER
That's a good boy. Fine boy. Fine, manly little fellow. Two thousand verses is a great many – A very, very great many. And you never can be sorry for the trouble you took to learn them; for knowledge is worth more than anything there is in the world. It's what makes men great and men. You'll be a great man and a good man yourself, some day, Thomas, and then you'll look back and say, 'It's all owing to the precious Sunday-school privileges of my boyhood. It's all owing to my dear teachers that taught me to learn. It's all owing to the good superintendent, who encouraged me, and watched over me, and gave me a beautiful Bible to keep and have all for my own, always. It's all owing to right bringing up!' That is what you will say, Thomas, and you wouldn't take any money for those two thousand verses. No, indeed you wouldn't.

And now, you wouldn't mind telling me and this lady some of the things you've learned? No doubt you know the names of all the twelve disciples. Won't you tell us the names of the first two that were appointed?

> (TOM was obviously not prepared for this turn of events, and stands mute.)

MR. WALTERS
Answer the gentleman, Thomas. Don't be afraid.

> (TOM still just stares at the floor.)

MRS. THATCHER
Now I know you'll tell me. The names of the first two disciples were...

TOM
David and Goliath!

> (Actors react, then freeze momentarily as
> MARK TWAIN enters. Then they begin
> changing the set to TOM'S Bedroom.)

MARK TWAIN
In charity, let us close this scene, as I am sure you can easily
imagine the outcome. After his inauspicious performance at the
Sunday School, Tom decided to retire early, and as a result,
awoke early the following morning in a state of pure misery.

It was Monday morning, and Monday morning always found
him so, because it began another week's slow suffering in
school. It occurred to him that he wished he was sick; then he
could stay home from school. He canvassed his system and
discovered he had a loose tooth. He was about to groan, when it
occurred to him that if he came into court with that argument, his
aunt would pull it out, and that would hurt. So he thought he
would hold the tooth in reserve for the present.

Then he remembered hearing the doctor tell about a certain thing
that laid up a patient for two or three weeks and threatened to
make him lose a finger. So the boy eagerly drew his sore toe
from under the sheet and held it up for inspection.

> (TWAIN exits. TOM begins to groan. SID
> continues to snore. TOM groans louder. SID
> sleeps on. Finally TOM shakes SID, and as he
> begins to rouse, groans even louder.)

SID
Tom! Say, Tom! Here, Tom! Tom! What is the matter, Tom?

TOM

Oh, don't, Sid. Don't joggle me.

SID

Why, what's the matter, Tom? I'll go git Aint Polly.

TOM

No. Never mind. It'll be over by and by, maybe. Don't git nobody.

SID

But I got to, Tom! Don't groan so. It's awful. How long you been this way?

TOM

Hours. Ouch! Oh, don't stir so, Sid, you'll kill me.

SID

Tom, why didn't you wake me sooner? Oh, Tom, don't! It makes my flesh crawl to hear you. Tom, what is the matter?

TOM

I forgive you everything, Sid. Everything you've ever done to me. When I'm gone...

SID

Oh, Tom, you ain't dying, are you?

TOM

I forgive everybody, Sid. Tell 'em so, Sid. And Sid, you give my window-sash and my cat with one eye to that new girl that's come to town, and tell her...

(SID rushes out hollering for all he's worth.)

SID
Aint Polly, Aint Polly! Come quick! Tom's dying!

AUNT POLLY
(From off stage.)
Dying!

SID
Yes'm. Don't wait! Come quick!

(AUNT POLLY, SID & MARY enter.)

AUNT POLLY
Rubbage! I don't believe it!

MARY
Tom! Tom, what's the matter?

TOM
Oh, Mary, I'm…

AUNT POLLY
What's the matter with you, Tom? Where do you hurt, child?

TOM
Oh, Aint Polly, my sore toe. It's mortified!

(AUNT POLLY & MARY look at each other as
if they should have known better, and burst out
laughing. SID begins to suspect TOM has
played him for a fool.)

AUNT POLLY
Tom, what a turn you did give me. Now you shut up that
nonsense and climb out of that bed.

TOM

Aint Polly, it seemed mortified, and it hurt so bad I never minded my tooth at all.

AUNT POLLY

Your tooth, indeed! What's the matter with your tooth?

TOM

One of them's loose, and it aches somethin' awful.

AUNT POLLY

Now, don't you commence to groaning again. Open your mouth. Well. Your tooth IS loose, but you're not going to die about that. Mary, get me a silk thread, and a chunk of fire out of the kitchen.

MARY

Yes'm.

(She exits.)

TOM

Oh, please, Aint Polly, don't pull it out. It don't hurt no more. Please? I don't want to stay home from school.

AUNT POLLY

Oh, you don't, do you? So all this row was because you thought you'd get to stay home from school and go a-fishing?

(MARY enters with some thread, a hot coal and a pair of tongs. AUNT POLLY makes one end of the silk thread fast to Tom's tooth with a loop and tied the other to the bedpost. Then she seized the coal and suddenly thrust it almost into TOM'S face. TOM starts to jerk back. Actors freeze for a moment while MARK TWAIN enters, then they begin setting the school.)

MARK TWAIN

Huckleberry Finn, whom you've already met, was son of the town drunk. He was cordially hated by all the mothers of the town, because he was idle and lawless and vulgar and bad; and because all their children admired him so, and delighted in his forbidden society, and wished they dared to be like him.

Huckleberry came and went at his own free will. He did not have to go to school or to church. He could go fishing or swimming when he chose, and stay as long as it suited him. He could sit up as late as he pleased. He was always the first boy that went barefoot in the spring and the last to resume shoe-leather in the fall. He never had to wash, nor put on clean clothes, and he could swear wonderfully. In a word, everything that goes to make life precious, that boy had. So thought every harassed, hampered, *respectable* boy in St. Petersburg.

> (TWAIN exits. TOM is busy studying the contents of a matchbox when he encounters HUCK.)

TOM

Hello, Huckleberry!

HUCK

Hello yourself, and see how you like it. What you got there?

TOM

It's a tick. First one of the season. Me and Ben Rogers are gonna race ticks at lunch time today at school. What's that you got?

HUCK

Dead cat.

TOM

Lemme see him, Huck. He's pretty stiff. Where'd you get him?

HUCK

Bought him off'n Jim Hooper.

TOM

What did you give?

HUCK

A blue ticket and a bladder that I got at the slaughter-house.

TOM

Where'd you get a blue ticket?

HUCK

Bought it off'n Ben Rogers two weeks ago for a hoop-stick.

TOM

Say, Huck. What is dead cats good for?

HUCK

Good for? Why, to cure warts with, o' course.

TOM

No! Is that so? I bet I know something that's better.

HUCK

I bet you don't. What?

TOM

Spunk-water.

HUCK

Spunk-water! I wouldn't give a pitcher of warm spit for spunk-water.

TOM

You wouldn't, huh? Didja ever try it?

HUCK
No, I hain't. But Bob Tanner did.

TOM
Who told you so?

HUCK
Well, Bob Tanner, he told Steve Walker, and Steve told Johnny Baker, and Johnny told Jim Hollis, and Jim told Ben Rogers, and Ben told Claude Herdman, and Claude told me. So there!

TOM
Well, that don't prove nuthin'. They'll all lie. Leastways all but that Herdman feller. I don't know him. But I know his brothers and sisters, and I ain't never seen a Herdman that wouldn't lie. Shucks! Now you tell me how Bob Tanner done it, Huck.

HUCK
Why, he took and dipped his hand in a rotten stump where the rain-water was.

TOM
In the daytime?

HUCK
Yes. Least I reckon so.

TOM
Did he say anything?

HUCK
No, I don't reckon he did.

TOM
Aha! Talk about trying to cure warts with spunk-water such a blame fool way as that! Why, that ain't a-going to do any good.

You got to go all by yourself, to the middle of the woods, where you know there's a spunk-water stump, and just as it's midnight you back up against the stump and jam your hand in and say:

'Barley-corn, barley-corn, wheat-meal shorts,
Spunk-water, spunk-water, swaller these warts!'

And then walk away quick, eleven steps, with your eyes shut, and then turn around three times and walk home without speaking to anybody. Because if you speak the charm's busted.

HUCK
Well, that ain't the way Bob Tanner done it.

TOM
No, sir, you can bet he didn't, becuz he's the wartiest boy in this town. Say, Huck, how do you cure warts with dead cats?

HUCK
You take your cat to the graveyard 'long about midnight when somebody wicked has been buried; and when it's midnight a devil will come, or maybe two or three, but you can't see 'em, you can only hear something like the wind, or maybe hear 'em talk; and when they're taking that feller away, you heave your cat after 'em and say, 'Devil follow corpse, cat follow devil, warts follow cat, I'm done with ye!' That'll fetch *any* wart.

TOM
Sounds right. Say, Huck, when you going to try the cat?

HUCK
Tonight. I reckon they'll come after old Hoss Williams tonight.

TOM
But they buried him Saturday. Didn't them devils get him Saturday night?

HUCK

Why, how you talk! How could their charms work till midnight? By by then it's Sunday. Devils don't slosh around much of a Sunday, I don't reckon.

TOM

I never thought of that. That's so. Can I go with you?

HUCK

'Course…if you ain't afeard.

TOM

Afeard! 'Tain't likely.

> (The boys separate as TOM enters the schoolroom, finds his place and sits.)

MR. WALTERS

Thomas Sawyer!

TOM

Sir?

MR. WALTERS

Late again, as usual. Would you mind explaining why?

TOM

> (Sees BECKY THATCHER and is so smitten
> that the inadvertently tells the truth.)

I stopped to talk with Huckleberry Finn.

MR. WALTERS

You…stopped to talk with Huckleberry Finn? Thomas Sawyer, this is the most astounding confession I have ever heard. No mere switching will answer for this offence. No, sir, you will go and sit with the girls!

(TOM pretends to be mortified, but makes his way to the only seat vacant, the one next to BECKY THATCHER.)

TOM

You're Becky Thatcher, ain't you? I saw you yesterday in Sunday School.

BECKY

And you are Thomas Sawyer. I saw *you* yesterday in Sunday School, too.

TOM

Thomas is the name they lick me by. I'm just Tom when I'm good.

(TOM writes on the slate.)

BECKY

What are you writing?

TOM

Oh, it ain't anything. You don't want to see.

BECKY

Yes I do, indeed I do. Please let me see.

TOM

You'll tell.

BECKY

No, I won't. Indeed and 'deed and double 'deed I won't.

TOM

You won't never tell nobody at all? As long as you live?

BECKY

No, I won't ever tell anybody. Now let me.

TOM

Oh, you don't want to see.

BECKY

Now that you treat me so, I will see!
                    (BECKY snatches the slate and reads.)
'I like you.' Oh, you bad thing!
                    (She slaps his hand, but looks pleased.)

MR. WALTERS

Thomas Sawyer! You may now return to your regular seat. And I hope you have learned your lesson.

                    (All actors freeze as MARK TWAIN enters, then they exit.)

MARK TWAIN

Noontime arrived and the school broke up for lunch, with groups of scholars of varying sizes wandering off to fill their stomachs and play while they may. All except Tom and Becky, who 'gave the rest of 'em the slip,' and returned to the now empty school room to spend, what you folks these days call, 'quality time' together.
                    (TOM and BECKY reenter.)

TOM

Do you like rats?

BECKY

No! I hate them!

TOM

Well, I do, too. Live ones. I mean dead ones, to swing round your head with a string.

BECKY

No, I don't care for rats much, alive or dead. What I like is chewing-gum.

TOM

Oh, I should say so! I wish I had some now.

BECKY

Do you? I've got some. I'll let you chew it awhile, but you must give it back to me.

TOM

Say, Becky, was you ever engaged?

BECKY

Engaged? What's that?

TOM

Why, engaged to be married, o' course.

BECKY

No.

TOM

Would you like to?

BECKY

I reckon so. I don't know. What is it like?

TOM

Like? Why it ain't like anything. You only just tell a boy you won't ever have anybody but him, and then you kiss and that's all. Anybody can do it.

BECKY
What do you kiss for?

TOM
Why, that, you know, is to - well, I don't rightly know. But they always do that when you get engaged.

BECKY
Everybody?

TOM
Why, yes, everybody. Do you remember what I wrote on the slate?

BECKY
No.

TOM
Then I'll whisper it to you.
(TOM leans in and whispers, "I like you.")
Now you got to whisper it to me, just the same.

BECKY
You turn your face away so you can't see, and then I will. But you mustn't ever tell anybody. Now you won't, will you?

TOM
No, indeed; indeed I won't.

(BECKY whispers her reply, and gives him a quick peck on the cheek.)

TOM
Now it's all done, Becky. And always after this, you ain't ever to

have nobody but me.

BECKY
And you ain't to ever marry anybody but me, either.

TOM
Certainly. Of course. That's part of it. And always coming to school or when we're going home, you're to walk with me when there ain't anybody looking; and you choose me and I choose you at parties, because that's the way you do when you're engaged.

BECKY
It's ever so nice. I never heard of it before.

TOM
Oh, it's ever so grand! Why, when me and Amy Lawrence was engaged...

BECKY
Oh, Tom! You mean I ain't the first one you've ever been engaged to?

TOM
Oh, don't cry, Becky, I don't care for her any more.

BECKY
Yes, you do, Tom. You know you do.

TOM
Becky, I...I don't care for anybody but you. Becky? Becky, won't you please say something?
> (Having no idea how to consol an emotional female, TOM decides to offer her his prized possession – a tick in a matchbox. He reaches into his pocket and retrieves the container.)

Becky, you can have my tick? Please, Becky, won't you take it?

> (BECKY strikes it to the floor. TOM, in total
> frustration, stalks out. BECKY realizes she has
> pushed TOM too far and rushes to the door.)

BECKY
Tom? Come back, Tom!

> (MARK TWAIN enters, and actors begin setting
> the stage for the graveyard scene.)

MARK TWAIN
At half-past nine that night, Tom and Sid were sent to bed. They said their prayers, and Sid was soon asleep. Tom, however, lay awake and waited in restless impatience. And then there came a most melancholy caterwauling. The raising of a neighboring window disturbed him. A cry of 'Scat, you devil!' and the crash of an empty bottle against the back of his aunt's woodshed brought him wide awake. A single minute later he was dressed, out of the window and creeping along the roof on all fours.

When he jumped to the ground, Huckleberry Finn was there, with his dead cat. The boys disappeared into the gloom. At the end of half an hour they were wading through the tall grass of the old graveyard.

The boys found the heap of fresh earth they were seeking, and ensconced themselves within the protection of three great elms that grew in a bunch within a few feet of the grave. There they waited in silence for midnight.

TOM
Huck, do you think the dead folks like for us to be here?

HUCK

I wisht I knowed. It's awful solemn like, ain't it?

TOM

Huck, do you reckon Hoss Williams hears us talking? I wish I'd said *Mister* Williams. But I never meant any harm. Everybody calls him Hoss.

HUCK

A body can't be too careful how they talk 'bout dead folks.

TOM

Sh!

HUCK

What is it, Tom?

TOM

Sh! There 'tis again! Didn't you hear it?

HUCK

Lord, Tom, they're coming! They're coming, sure. What'll we do?

TOM

I dunno. Think they'll see us?

HUCK

Oh, Tom, they can see in the dark, same as cats. I wisht I hadn't come.

TOM

Maybe they won't bother us. We ain't doing any harm. If we keep perfectly still, maybe they won't notice us at all.

HUCK

I'll try, Tom, but, Lordy, I'm all a shiver.

TOM

Look! Over there! What's that?

HUCK

It's devil-fire. Oh, Tom, this is awful. It's devils sure enough. Three of 'em! Lordy, Tom, we're goners! Can you pray?

TOM

I'll try. Now I lay me down to sleep, I...

> (MUFF POTTER, INJUN JOE, AND DR. ROBINSON can be heard muttering from offstage.)

HUCK

Sh!

TOM

What is it, Huck?

HUCK

Those ain't devils. They're humans! One of 'em is, anyway. That's Muff Potter's voice. Don't you stir. He ain't sharp enough to notice us. More'n likely drunk, the same as usual.

TOM

Say, Huck, I know another o' them voices. It's Injun Joe.

HUCK

That murderin' varmint? I'd druther they was devils a dern sight. What d'you figure they be up to?

> (MUFF POTTER, INJUN JOE, AND DR.

    ROBINSON enter, carrying shovels, a lantern,
    and pushing a wheelbarrow.)

DR. ROBINSON

Here it is. Hurry. The moon might come out at any moment.

MUFF POTTER

    (Speech is slurred, obviously drunk. He pulls out
    his knife and starts peeling an apple.)

We'll dig up the body for you, Sawbones, but it's gonna cost you
another five.

DR. ROBINSON

Look here, you required your pay in advance, and I've paid you
already.

INJUN JOE

Well, it's another five, or you can dig up the corpse yourself.

    (DR. ROBINSON is not cowed. He strikes out
    suddenly, knocking INJUN JOE to the ground.
    MUFF is startled, drops his knife and apple, and
    tries to intervene.)

MUFF POTTER

Here, now, don't you hit my pard!

    (MUFF and DR. ROBINSON grapple for a
    moment. INJUN JOE recovers and picks up
    MUFF'S knife. DR. ROBINSON shoves MUFF
    away. MUFF falls and hits his head against a
    gravestone. INJUN JOE lunges forward,
    stabbing DR. ROBINSON to death, then places
    the knife in MUFF'S hand as MUFF begins to
    rouse.)

MUFF

Oh, Lordy, what happened here, Joe?

INJUN JOE

It's a dirty business. What did you do it for?

MUFF

Me? I never done it. Did I?
(He drops the knife beside the body.)

INJUN JOE

You two was scuffling, and he knocked you into a gravestone; and then up you come, all reeling and staggering like, and snatched the knife and jammed it into him, just as he fetched you another awful clip. Here you've laid, as dead as a wedge til now.

MUFF

I didn't know what I was a-doing. I wish I may die this minute if I did. It was all on account of the whiskey, I reckon. Joe, don't tell! Say you won't tell, Joe. That's a good feller. I always liked you, Joe, and stood up for you, too. Don't you remember? You won't tell, will you, Joe?

INJUN JOE

No, you've always been fair and square with me, Muff, and I won't go back on you. But this ain't the time for loitering. You be off yonder way and I'll go this. Move, now, and don't leave any tracks behind you.

(MUFF and INJUN JOE run off in opposite directions. Once the men are gone the boys take off running. The lights fade to black. When the lights rise, the boys are outside of TOM'S house.)

TOM

Huckleberry, what do you reckon'll come of this?

HUCK

I reckon hangin'll come of it.

TOM

Do you think we oughta tell?

HUCK

What are you talking about? S'pose something happened and Injun Joe didn't hang? Why, he'd kill us both dead, just as sure as we're standing here. Let Muff Potter tell.

TOM

Muff Potter don't know. He'd just got that whack when Injun Joe done it. I don't reckon he knowed anything.

HUCK

By hokey, that's so, Tom. And besides, he was all liquored up.

TOM

Huck, you sure you can keep mum?

HUCK

Tom, we *got* to keep mum. That devil wouldn't think any more of drownding us than a couple of cats. Now, look-a-here, Tom, let's take and swear to one another. That's what we got to do - swear to keep mum.

TOM

I'm agreed. It's the best thing. We should just hold hands and swear that we...

HUCK

Oh no, that wouldn't do for this. That's good enough for little rubbishy common things; specially with gals, 'cuz they go back on you anyway, and blab if they get in a huff. But for a big thing like this, there orta be blood.

>(TOM nods and pulls his sure 'nuff Barlow knife out and he and HUCK make a small incision on their thumbs. They press their thumbs together.)

TOM
Tom Sawyer and Huck Finn swears they will keep mum about this and they wish they may drop down dead in their tracks if they ever tell and rot.

HUCK
I'm agreed.

TOM
You want to sleep on the porch tonight, Huck?

HUCK
I'd be obleeged, Tom.

>(Lights fade. Spot on MARK TWAIN.)

MARK TWAIN
Good news will keep, the saying goes, but bad news flies on the wings of the wind. Long before nine the following day the whole village was a-buzz with the ghastly news. A gory knife had been found close to the murdered Doctor, and somebody recognized it as belonging to Muff Potter.

Muff was apprehended and confessed to grave robbing for the young doctor. Injun Joe told his version of the unfortunate events and the upshot was that Injun Joe walked free while Muff Potter was thrown in the county jail to await trial for murder. For many days after, Tom wrestled with a guilty conscience.

(Spot fades on MARK TWAIN. Lights up inside
AUNT POLLY'S house. TOM, AUNT POLLY,
SID, AND MARY are having breakfast.)

SID

Tom, you pitched around and talked in your sleep so much that
you kept me awake half the night.

AUNT POLLY

It's a bad sign. What you got on your mind, Tom?

TOM

Nothing. Nothing I know of.

SID

And you talked such stuff. Last night you said, 'It's blood, it's
blood, that's what it is!' You said that over and over. And you
said, 'Don't torment me so - I'll tell!' Tell what?

AUNT POLLY

Sho! It's that dreadful murder trial. It's been going on all week
and it is all anybody talks of. I dream about it 'most every night
myself. Sometimes I dream it's me that done it.

MARY

Why, it has affected me much the same way. Somehow, I just
can't believe old Muff Potter capable of doing such a dastardly
deed. He's always been such a harmless, pathetic old man.

AUNT POLLY

It's the drink that made him do it. Let that be a lesson to
everyone in this town. Whisky is the devil's tool. Muff Potter'll
hang for this, you mark my words.

MARY

It's so sad. Jeff Thatcher is defending him, and Lawyer Thatcher is a good man. But I heard he hasn't asked a single question to a single witness, and this is the last day of the trial. I don't think he's even trying to defend Muff Potter.

SID
I hear their going to put Injun Joe on the stand today. That'll sink if for old Muff.

TOM
Aint Polly, might'n I be excused? I don't feel much like eating.

> (TOM walks outside as the rest of the cast freezes momentarily, then begin setting up the jail/court. Once outside, TOM encounters HUCK.)

TOM
Huck, have you ever told anybody about…that?

HUCK
Why, Tom Sawyer, we wouldn't be alive two days if that got found out. You know that.

TOM
Well, all right, then. I reckon we're safe as long as we keep mum. What's the talk around, Huck?

HUCK
Talk? Well, it's just Muff Potter, Muff Potter, Muff Potter all the time. It keeps me in a sweat, constant, so's I want to hide som'ers.

TOM
That's just the same way they go on round me. I reckon he's a goner. Don't you feel sorry for him, sometimes?

HUCK

Most always. He ain't no account; but then he hain't ever done anything to hurt anybody. Just fishes a little, to get money to get drunk on. And loafs around considerable; but lord, we all do that, leastways most of us. But he give me half a fish, once, when there warn't enough for two.

TOM

Well, he's mended kites for me, Huck, and knitted hooks on to my line. I wish we could get him out of there.

HUCK

We cain't get him out, Tom. And besides, 'twouldn't do any good; they'd just ketch him again.

> (The boys arrive at the back of the county jail. MUFF is looking through the barred window. HUCK and TOM pass his some tobacco and matches. The remainder of the cast begins to fill the courtroom.)

MUFF

You've been mighty good to me, boys, better'n anybody else in this town. And I don't forget it, I don't. Often I says to myself, says I, 'I used to mend all the boys' kites and things, and show 'em where the good fishin' places was, and now they've all forgot old Muff when he's in trouble. But Tom don't, and Huck don't. 'They don't forget him,' says I, 'and I don't forget them.' Well, boys, I done an awful thing. Drunk and crazy at the time, that's the only way I account for it, and now I got to swing for it, and it's right. Right, and best, too, I reckon. Hope so, anyway.

Well, we won't talk about that. I don't want to make you feel bad. But what I want to say is, don't you ever get drunk; then you won't ever get here. I tell you, it's a prime comfort to see faces that's friendly when a body's in such trouble.

(JEFF THATCHER enters the jail to escort MUFF to the courtroom. TOM and HUCK run to the courtroom and squeeze their way in. JUDGE THATCHER is presiding. MR. WALTERS is acting as bailiff.)

JEFF

It's time, Muff.

(Once JEFF and MUFF are seated the proceedings begin.)

PROSECUTOR

I call Injun Joe to the stand.

MR. WALTERS

Do you swear to tell the truth, the whole truth, and nothing but the truth, so help you God?

INJUN JOE

I do.

PROSECUTOR

Now, sir. Will you tell the court what happened on the night Dr. Robinson was murdered?

INJUN JOE

Doc Robinson paid me and Muff five dollars to dig up Hoss Williams body. Muff and me, we got to thinkin' – it ain't right disturbin' the dead. Oughta be worth more'n five dollars. Muff asked Doc Robinson for another five, and he went crazy. Knock me down, then went after Muff. They went to scuffling, and he knocked Muff into a gravestone. I thought he'd killed him, but then Muff come up, all reeling and staggering like, and snatched up his knife and jammed it into the Doc.

PROSECUTOR
Your witness.

JEFF THATCHER
No questions.

JUDGE THATCHER
Jeff, is it your intention to let your client go to the gallows without asking a single question?

JEFF THATCHER
If it please the court, I'll save my questions for the defense.

PROSECUTOR
Then by the oaths of citizens whose simple word is above suspicion, we have fastened this crime, beyond all possibility of question, upon the unhappy prisoner at the bar. The state rests.

JEFF THATCHER
Your honor, in our remarks at the opening of this trial, we foreshadowed our purpose to prove that our client did this fearful deed while under the influence of a blind and irresponsible delirium produced by drink. We have changed our mind. We shall not offer that plea. I call to the stand...Thomas Sawyer!

(TOM approaches the witness stand.)

MR. WALTERS
Thomas, do you swear to tell the truth, the whole truth, and nothing but the truth, so help you God?

TOM
I do.

JUDGE THATCHER
Thomas, do you understand that you are under oath?

TOM
Yes, sir.

JUDGE THATCHER
That is an awful, solemn oath, Thomas. Do you understand what it means?

TOM
It means I got to tell the truth, and if I lie I'll burn in Hell forever and ever.

JUDGE THATCHER
I do believe the boy understands the seriousness of his testimony. Jeff, you may proceed with your questions.

JEFF THATCHER
Thomas Sawyer, where were you on the seventeenth of June, about the hour of midnight?

TOM
In the graveyard.

JEFF THATCHER
A little bit louder, please. Don't be afraid. You were...

TOM
In the graveyard.

JEFF THATCHER
Were you anywhere near Hoss Williams' grave?

TOM
Yes, sir.

JEFF THATCHER
Speak up just a trifle louder. How near were you?

TOM

Near as I am to you.

JEFF THATCHER

Were you hidden, or not?

TOM

I was hid. Behind the elms that's on the edge of the grave.

JEFF THATCHER

Any one with you?

TOM

Yes, sir.

JEFF THATCHER

Who?

TOM

I 'druther not say. We swore an oath not to tell.

JEFF THATCHER

Did you carry anything there with you? Speak out, my boy. don't be afraid. The truth is always respectable.

TOM

Only a...a...dead cat.

> (Laughter from the crowd. JUDGE THATCHER calls them to order.)

JEFF THATCHER

We will produce the skeleton of that cat. Now, my boy, tell us everything that occurred. Tell it in your own way. Don't skip anything.

TOM

Well, me and Hu…, me and this other feller, went out to the graveyard. We had this dead cat 'cause we were going to use it to take off warts. 'Long about midnight we saw three fellers coming our way, and we got scared and hid. When they got close enough we could tell it was Doctor Robinson, Muff Potter and Injun Joe. Well, those three men commenced to fightin' and Doc Robinson knocked Muff plumb out. That's when Injun Joe jumped at him with the knife and…

INJUN JOE

I'm gonna kill you, boy!

> (INJUN JOE immediate bursts out of the courtroom and is gone before anyone can think to stop him.)

> (BLACKOUT. END OF ACT I)

ACT II

SETTING: The Courtroom.

AT RISE: Actors in costume begin setting the stage with the haunted house scene home. HUCKLEBERRY FINN notices the audience and steps forward. He looks around to make sure MARK TWAIN is nowhere around. Satisfied, he addresses the audience.

HUCK
Howdy again. It's me, Huckleberry. After the trial, Tom was treated like a glitterin' hero. Why, he even got his name in the newspaper. I heard tell Jeff Thatcher said he believed Tom might make President, yet, if he escaped hanging. I was mighty glad Muff didn't hang, and I suppose I woulda told if Tom hadn't. But I'm just as glad it was him and not me. I cain't stand that much attention.

Tom, he was all puffed up over being the town favorite. Least-wise during the daytime. But night times were a torment to him.

MARK TWAIN
Huckleberry.

HUCK
The lights was up and these folks were just sittin' here and I didn't see you nowhere's...

MARK TWAIN

Run along, Huckleberry. I believe you have a large part in the next scene.

(HUCK exits.)

MARK TWAIN

As my young friend was saying, while Tom's days were full of splendor and exultation, his nights were seasons of horror. Injun Joe infested all his dreams, and always with doom in his eye. Hardly any temptation could persuade the boy to stir abroad after nightfall.

Life does not stand still, however, even in a small town, and in youth there abides an unquenchable optimism. Eventually, Tom's enthusiasm for adventure overcame his fear of Injun Joe, and once again he ventured forth.

Now, there comes a time in every rightly-constructed boy's life when he has a raging desire to go somewhere and dig for hidden treasure. This desire suddenly came upon Tom one day. He stumbled upon Huck Finn, and took him to a private place and opened the matter to him confidentially. Huck was willing, for he had a troublesome super-abundance of that sort of time which is *not* money.

(TWAIN exits. TOM and HUCK wander in carrying a shovel and pick.)

HUCK

Who is it that hides all this buried treasure?

TOM

Why, robbers, of course. Who'd you reckon? Preachers?

HUCK

I don't know. If 'twas mine I wouldn't hide it; I'd spend it.

TOM

So would I. But robbers don't do that way. They always hide it and leave it there.

HUCK

Don't they come after it any more?

TOM

No. They think they will, but they generally forget the marks, or else they die. Anyway, it lays there a long time and gets rusty; and by and by somebody finds an old yellow paper that tells how to find the marks - a paper that's got to be ciphered over about a week because it's mostly signs and hy'roglyphics.

HUCK

Hyro-which-its?

TOM

Hy'roglyphics. Pictures and things, you know, that don't seem to mean anything.

HUCK

Have you got one of them papers, Tom?

TOM

No.

HUCK

Well how you going to find the marks?

TOM

I don't need any marks. They always bury it under a hainted house or on an island, or under a dead tree that's got one limb sticking out. Well, we've tried Jackson's Island a little, and there's the old hainted house up the Still-House branch, and there's lots of deadlimb trees - dead loads of 'em.

HUCK
Is it under all of them?

TOM
Of course not.

HUCK
Then how you going to know which one to go for?

TOM
Go for all of 'em.

HUCK
Tom, it'll take all year.

TOM
Well, what of that? Suppose you find a brass pot with a hundred dollars in it, all rusty and gray, or a rotten chest full of di'monds.

HUCK
Just you gimme the hundred dollars. I don't want no di'monds.

TOM
All right. But you'll wish you didn't throw off them di'monds. Some of 'em's worth twenty dollars apiece. There ain't any, hardly, but's worth six bits or a dollar.

HUCK
No? Is that so?

TOM
Cert'nly. Anybody'll tell you so. Say, Huck, when we find a

treasure, what you going to do with your share?

HUCK
I'll have pie and a glass of soda every day, and I'll go to every circus that comes along.

TOM
I'm going to buy a new drum, and a sure-'nough sword, and a red necktie and a bull pup, and get married.

HUCK
Married?! Tom, you ain't in your right mind. That's the foolishest thing you could do. Look at pap and my mother, back when she was alive. Fight? Why, they used to fight all the time.

TOM
Well, the girl I'm going to marry won't fight.

HUCK
Tom, they're all alike. Now you better think 'bout this awhile. I tell you, you better. 'Sides, if you get married I'll be more lonesomer than ever.

TOM
No, you won't. You'll come and live with me. Now let's get to digging. Look sharp, Huck. They 'most always put in a dead man when they bury a treasure under a tree, to look out for it.

HUCK
Lordy! Tom, I don't like to fool around much where there's dead folks. A body's bound to get into trouble with 'em. S'pose this one here was to stick his skull out and say something. It'd be awful! Tom, let's give this place up, and try some'rs else.

TOM
We could try the hainted house.

HUCK

Blame it, I don't like hainted houses either, Tom. Why, they're a dern sight worser'n dead folks. Dead folks might talk, maybe, but they don't come sliding around in a shroud, when you ain't noticing, and peep over your shoulder all of a sudden and grit their teeth, the way a ghost does. I couldn't stand such a thing as that, Tom.

TOM

But, Huck, ghosts only travel around at night. They won't hinder us from digging there in the daytime. Anyhow, ain't nobody ever seen nuthin' around that house, 'cept just some blue lights slipping by the windows - no regular ghosts.

HUCK

Where you see one of them blue lights flickering around, you can bet there's a ghost mighty close behind it. It stands to reason. Becuz you know that they don't anybody but ghosts use 'em.

TOM

Yes, that's so. But they don't come around in the daytime, so what's the use of our being afeard?

HUCK

Well, all right. We'll tackle the hainted house if you say so. But I reckon it's still taking chances.

> (TOM and HUCK enter the house. They put their shovel and pick down in the corner and begin to explore. They see a closet and dare each other to open it. They hear a noise that startles them.)

TOM

Sh! Did you hear that?

HUCK

Yes. Oh, lordy, let's run!

TOM

Keep still. They're coming right toward the door. Into the closet, quick!

> (The boys hide in the closet. INJUN JOE enters along with PARD.)

PARD

No. I've thought it all over, and it's too dangerous.

INJUN JOE

Dangerous? Milksop! What's any more dangerous than that job up yonder, but nothin's come of that.

PARD

That's different. That was way up the river, and not another house about.

INJUN JOE

Well, what's more dangerous than coming here in the daytime? Anybody would suspicion us that saw us.

PARD

I know that. But there warn't any other place. I want to quit this shantytown. I wished we was gone yesterday.

INJUN JOE

You go back up the river and wait there till you hear from me. I'll take the chance on dropping into town once more. We'll do that 'dangerous' job after I've spied around a bit. Then we're off for Texas. What'll we do with what little swag we've got left?

PARD

Leave it here as we've always done, I reckon. No use takin' it till we start south. Six hundred and fifty in silver's a lot to carry.

INJUN JOE

All right. It won't matter to come here once more. But look here; it may be a good while before I get the right chance at that job; accidents might happen; 'tain't in such a very good place; we'll just bury it, and bury it deep.

PARD

I'm agreed.

INJUN JOE

I need something to pry up this floor board. I saw an old pick in the corner. We'll make quick work of it.

> (PARD hands him the pick. INJUN JOE looks at it curiously for a moment, as if something is amiss, then pries up a floor board.)

INJUN JOE

Hello, what have we here?

> (INJUN JOE pulls up an old strong box. He pops off the rusted lock and opens the box revealing lots of coins.)

Pard, there's thousands of dollars here.

PARD

'Twas always said that Murrel's gang used to be around here one summer. Looks like we found their stash. Now you won't need to do that job.

INJUN JOE

You don't know me, Pard. Least you don't know all about me. 'Tain't robbery I'm after. It's revenge! And I'll need your help.

We don't leave til it's finished.

PARD
If you say so. What'll we do with this, bury it again?

INJUN JOE
Yes. No! I just realized what bothered me about that pick. It had fresh earth on it. What business has a pick and a shovel here? Bury it again and leave them to come and see the ground disturbed? No, sir. We'll take it to my den. Number Two, under the cross.

PARD
All right. It's dark enough to start.

> (INJUN JOE and PARD exit, taking the money with them. The boys cautiously creep out.)

TOM
Revenge? I think he means us, Huck.

HUCK
He don't know about me, Tom. I think he means you!

> (Actors freeze momentarily, then begin setting AUNT POLLY'S home. MARK TWAIN enters.)

MARK TWAIN
Once again Tom spent his days imagining Injun Joe hiding behind every tree and bush. But as each day drifted inexorably into the next day, Tom's sense of foreboding gradually lightened, until soon he rarely thought of Injun Joe at all. All in all it was a carefree time for Tom, although he frequently got into trouble, which is the primary purpose of young boys upon this earth.

On one such occasion, when he was feeling particularly put upon, Tom determined to take arms against a sea of outrageous fortune. He decided to run away.

> (MARK TWAIN exits. TOM is sitting in front of the fence when JOE HARPER walks up in great distress.)

TOM

I 'low if I was drowned they'd be sorry. They'd cry over me, and beg me to forgive 'em, but it'd be too late. I'd be dead and gone and never come back. They'd be sorry then. I've half a mind to roam abroad into the great world, never to return.

JOE

I know just what you mean, Tom. My Ma, she just whipped me for drinking some cream, which I swear I never tasted. It's plain she's tired of me and wishes for me to go. Well, if she feels that way, there's nuthin' for me to do but leave. I hope she'll be happy and never regret having driven her poor boy out into the unfeeling world to suffer and die.

TOM

It's a cruel world Joe, that's so. Where you thinkin' about going?

JOE

I'm all for being a hermit, and living on crusts of bread in a remote cave, and dying sometime of cold and want and grief. How 'bout you?

TOM

Being a hermit is all well and good, but it ain't shucks to a life of crime. I'm figurin' on being a pirate.

> (HUCK approaches.)

HUCK

What d'you want to be a pirate for?

TOM

It's just the life for me. You don't have to get up mornings, and you don't have to go to school, and wash, and all that blame foolishness. A pirate don't have to do anything when he's ashore. Joe was all for being a hermit, but a hermit, he has to be praying considerable, and then he don't have any fun, all by himself that way.

JOE

Yes, that's so. I hadn't thought much about it, you know. I'd a good deal rather be a pirate, now I think about it.

TOM

People don't go much on hermits, nowadays, not like they used to in old times. He's got to sleep on the hardest place he can find, and put sackcloth and ashes on his head, and stand out in the rain, and...

HUCK

What does he put sackcloth and ashes on his head for?

TOM

I dunno. But they've got to do it. Hermits always do. You'd have to do that if you was a hermit, Huck.

HUCK

Dern'd if I would.

JOE

Why, Huck, you'd have to. How'd you get around it?

HUCK

Why, I just wouldn't stand fer it. I'd run away.

JOE

Run away?! Well, you would be a nice old slouch of a hermit.

HUCK

So, what does pirates have to do?

TOM

Oh, they have just a grand time. They take ships and burn them, and get the money and bury it in awful places on their island where there's ghosts and such to watch over it, and make everbody in the ships walk the plank.

JOE

And don't they wear the grandest clothes! All gold and silver and di'monds.

HUCK

I reckon I ain't dressed fittin' for a pirate. But I ain't got none but these.

TOM

Oh, Huck, the fine clothes will come fast enough, after we start taking ships. What you got on will do to begin with.

> (Actors freeze momentarily as MARK TWAIN enters. The cast begins to set the opposite side of the stage for The Island.)

MARK TWAIN

Three miles below St. Petersburg, at a point where the Mississippi River is a trifle over a mile wide, there is a long, narrow, wooded island which is wholly unpeopled. To the boys' minds, Jackson's Island was the ideal spot to begin their career as pirates. Who were to be the subjects of their piracies was a matter that did not occur to them.

About midnight Tom Sawyer, the Black Avenger of the Spanish Main, arrived at the prescribed meeting place with a boiled ham. He was soon joined by Huck Finn the Red-Handed, and Joe Harper the Terror of the Seas, titles furnished by Tom from his favorite literature. The Terror of the Seas had brought a side of bacon, and had about worn himself out with getting it there. Finn the Red-Handed had stolen a skillet, a quantity of leaf tobacco, and a few corn-cobs to make pipes with, although none of the pirates smoked or chewed but himself.

Tom's raft provided easy access to Jackson's Island, and before long they were comfortably lodged in the depths of the island's forest, with a pleasant fire and bacon sizzling in the frying pan.

> (MARK TWAIN exits. TOM, HUCK, and JOE are lounging around the fire.)

JOE
Ain't this grand?

TOM
What would the boys say if they could see us?

JOE
Say? Well, they'd just die to be here, hey, Hucky?

HUCK
I reckon so. I'm suited. I don't want nothing better'n this. But lookie here, fellers. I'm bushed. I think I'm gonna turn in.

> (HUCK pulls his hat down over his eyes and almost immediately drifts off to sleep. TOM and JOE continue to talk in hushed tones.)

JOE
Tom, do you figure pirates kneel down and say their prayers

before getting to sleep?

TOM
I think pirates mainly say their prayers to themselves.

JOE
Yeah, you're probably right. Say, Tom, you figure it might have been wrong of us to take that ham and bacon?

TOM
Shucks, Joe. We've hooked apples and sweetmeats before, lots of times.

JOE
Yeah, that's so. But Tom, that was only hooking. Bacon and hams and such are valuables and that makes it stealing. And there is a command against that in the Bible.

TOM
That's so. I tell you what, we'll go ahead and say our prayers to ourselves, and we'll not let our piracies be sullied again with the crime of stealing. How's that?

JOE
That's fine, Tom. Good night, Tom.

TOM
Good night, Joe.

> (Lights fade. When they rise there is a sound of cannon fire in the distance, which wakes the boys.)

JOE
I wonder what it is?

HUCK

'Tain't thunder, becuz thunder...

TOM

Hush! Listen...don't talk...Let's go and see.

> (The boys move to the edge of their campsite where they can see the river. More 'booms' are heard.)

TOM

I know what it is. Somebody's drownded!

HUCK

That's it. They done that last summer, when Bill Turner got drownded; they shoot a cannon over the water, and that makes him come up to the top.

JOE

I'd give heaps to know who it is who's drowned.

TOM

I know who's drownded. It's us!

HUCK

Us?

JOE

O' course. Us! Why, this is fine, Tom. This is just a triumph, that's what this is. We're missed and mourned. Hearts are breakin' on our account, and tears are being shed. I just bet they're thinking about all the times they was mean and unkind, and regrettin' it heaps.

TOM

Yessir, boys. It's worth it being pirates after all. Don't you know the boys back home just wishes they was here.

JOE
I just bet they do. Say, boys, piratin' is hungry work. Let's go back to camp and have some more of that bacon.

> (Lights dim and rise several times, each time revealing the boys in a different position. It should be clear by the last time that they are beginning to get more than a little bored and homesick. Finally the lights rise as HUCK puts the finishing touches on a corncob pipe. He hands one to TOM and another to JOE.)

TOM
Thank ye, Huck. I've been wanting to learn to smoke.

> (TOM and JOE watch HUCK tamp the tobacco into his pipe and light it with a stick from the fire, and they copy his movements. There is considerable coughing and gagging from the beginners.)

TOM
Why, it's just as easy! If I'd a knowed this was all, I'd a learnt long ago.

JOE
So would I. It's just nothing.

TOM
Why, many a time I've looked at people smoking, and thought, 'I wish I could do that,' but I never thought I could.

JOE
That's just the way with me. I bleeve I could smoke this pipe all

day. I don't feel sick at all.

TOM

Neither do I. I *could* smoke it all day. But I bet you Ben Rogers couldn't.

JOE

Ben Rogers! Why, he'd keel over just with two draws. Just let him try it once. He'd see.

TOM

'Deed it would, Joe. Say, I wish the boys could see us now.

> (During this entire conversation both boys are getting greener around the gills. Despite their bravado, by now they are seriously sick.)

JOE

I've...uh... I think I've lost my knife. I reckon I better go and find it.

TOM

I'll help you. You go over that way and I'll hunt around by the spring. No, you needn't come, Huck. We can find it.

> (TOM and JOE exit in opposite directions, and soon after HUCK hears the sound of retching coming from both directions. He begins to laugh. Lights fade, then rise. HUCK and JOE are fast asleep. TOM rises, makes sure his friends are asleep, then exits. Lights fade out on the Island, and rise on AUNT POLLY'S home. AUNT POLLY, SID, MARY, & MRS. HARPER are talking. TOM has just sneaked in through the back door.)

AUNT POLLY

But as I was saying, he warn't bad, so to say, only mischeevous. Only just giddy, and harum-scarum, you know. He warn't any more responsible than a colt.

MRS. HARPER

It was just so with my Joe. Always full of his devilment, and up to every kind of mischief, but he was just as unselfish and kind as he could be. And laws bless me, to think I went and whipped him for taking that cream, never once recollecting that I throwed it out my own self because it was sour.

SID

I hope Tom's better off where he is, but if he'd been better in some ways...

MARY

Sid! Not a word against Tom, now that he's gone. God'll take care of him, never you trouble yourself, sir.

AUNT POLLY

Oh, Sereny, I don't know how to give him up. He was such a comfort to me, although he 'most tormented my old heart out of me.

MRS. HARPER

The Lord giveth and the Lord hath taken away. Blessed be the name of the Lord! But it's so hard. Only last Saturday my Joe busted a firecracker right under my nose and I knocked him sprawling. Little did I know then, how soon...Oh, if it was to do over again I'd hug him and bless him for it.

AUNT POLLY

I know just how you feel, Sereny. No longer ago than three days ago, my Tom took and filled the cat full of Pain-killer, and I did think the critter would tear the house down. And God forgive

me, I cracked Tom's head with my thimble. But he's out of all
his troubles now.

MRS. HARPER
I have to leave now Polly. I'll see you at the funeral in the
morning.

> (MRS. HARPER exits amidst much sobbing all
> around. AUNT POLLY, MARY and SID all
> retire for the night. TOM creeps into the sitting
> room, finds a pencil and some paper, and begins
> to write a note, reading aloud as he does so.)

TOM
Dear Aint Polly. Don't worry. We ain't dead. We're only off
playing pirates. Tom.

> (TOM leaves the note where it will be found and
> starts to leave. Suddenly an idea occurs to him.
> He turns and picks up the note, folds it, and puts
> it in his jacket pocket, and leaves. MARK
> TWAIN enters, and cast members begin clearing
> the Island, and setting the church scene. Once
> set, cast members begin to make their way into
> the pews.)

MARK TWAIN
While our band of pirates was having a fine time, there was no
hilarity in the little town. The Harpers and Aunt Polly's family
were put into mourning, with great grief and many tears. An
unusual quiet possessed the village. It's inhabitants conducted
their concerns with an absent air. They talked little; but sighed
often.

A group of boys and girls came by, and stood looking over the
whitewashed fence. There was a dispute about who saw the dead

boys last in life, and who exchanged the last words with them. One poor chap, who had no other grandeur to offer, said with tolerably pride in the remembrance: 'Well, Tom Sawyer, he licked me once.'

But that bid for glory was a failure as most of the other boys could say the same. When the appointed day for the funeral arrived, it seemed the church bell tolled, instead of ringing in its usual way. The congregation gathered, filling the little church to a capacity it had not seen in many a year.

> (MARK TWAIN joins the congregation, which has risen during TWAIN'S monologue, and has been softly singing a hymn. The volume increases when TWAIN finishes. MR. WALTERS moves to the podium.)

MR. WALTERS
I am the Resurrection and the Life. He who believes in me, though he were dead, yet shall he live again…

> (There is a rustling in the back of the church, as the three boys start to walk down the aisle. There is a startled silence then pandemonium breaks out. HUCK, who has no family there, hangs back and tries to slink away.)

TOM
Aint Polly, it ain't fair. Somebody's got to be glad to see Huck.

AUNT POLLY
And so they shall. I'm glad to see him, poor motherless thing!

MR. WALTERS
Praise God from whom all blessings flow! SING! And put your hearts in it!

(The congregation takes up the Doxology with great gusto as the lights fade on the church. Lights rise on AUNT POLLY'S home. TOM, AUNT POLLY, MARY and SID are having breakfast.)

AUNT POLLY

Well, I don't say it wasn't a fine joke, Tom, to keep everybody suffering 'most a week so you boys could have a good time. But it is a pity you could be so hard-hearted as to let me suffer so. If you could come over on a log to go to your own funeral, you could have come over and give me a hint some way that you warn't dead.

MARY

Yes, you could have done that, Tom, and I believe you would if you had thought of it.

AUNT POLLY

It would have been something if you'd cared enough to think of it, even if you didn't do it.

MARY

Now, auntie, you know it's only Tom's giddy way. He is always in such a rush that he never thinks of anything.

AUNT POLLY

More's the pity. Sid would have thought. And Sid would have done it, too. Tom, you'll look back, some day, when it's too late, and wish you'd cared a little more for me when it would have cost you so little.

TOM

Now, Aint Polly, you know I do care for you.

AUNT POLLY

I'd know it better if you acted more like it.

TOM

I wish now I'd thought about it. But I dreamt about you. That's something, ain't it?

AUNT POLLY

It ain't much. A cat does that much. What did you dream?

TOM

Why, it were night before last. I dreamt that you was sitting over there, and Sid was sitting by you, and Mary next to him. And I dreamt that Joe Harper's mother was here.

AUNT POLLY

Why, that's just the way it was. Did you dream any more?

TOM

Somehow it seems to me that the wind... the wind blowed the candle.

AUNT POLLY

Mercy on us! Go on, Tom.

TOM

And it seems to me that you said, 'Why, I believe that door was open,' and it seems like you made Sid go and shut it.

AUNT POLLY

I never heard the beat of that in all my born days! Don't tell me there ain't anything in dreams. Sereny Harper shall know of this before I'm an hour older. I'd like to see her get around this with her rubbage 'bout superstition. Go on, Tom.

TOM

Next you said I warn't bad, only mischeevous and harum-scarum. And then you began to cry.

AUNT POLLY

So I did. Not the first time, neither.

TOM

Then Mrs. Harper she began to cry, and said Joe was just the same, and she wished she hadn't whipped him for taking cream when she'd throwed it out her own self.

AUNT POLLY

Tom! The sperrit was upon you! You was a prophesying, that's what you was doing!

TOM

Then Sid he said…

SID

I don't think I said anything.

MARY

Yes, you did, Sid.

TOM

He said he hoped I was better off where I was gone to, but if I'd been better sometimes…

AUNT POLLY

It was his very words!

TOM

And Mrs. Harper told about Joe scaring her with a firecracker, and you told about the cat and the painkiller and then there was a whole lot of talk 'bout dragging the river for us, and 'bout having the funeral Sunday, and then you and Mrs. Harper hugged and cried, and she went home. Then you went to bed, and I was so sorry that I took and wrote on a piece of paper, 'We ain't dead - we are only off being pirates,' and put it on the table.

SID
That was very kind...even though it was only a dream.

AUNT POLLY
Hush up, Sid! A body does just the same in a dream as he'd do if he was awake. Now go 'long to school. I'm thankful to the good God and Father of us all that's long-suffering and merciful to them that believe on Him and keep His word, I've got you back, though goodness knows I'm unworthy of it. But if only the worthy ones got His blessings and had His hand to help them over the rough places, there's few enough would smile here or ever enter into His rest when the long night comes. Go 'long Sid, Mary, Tom. You've hindered me long enough.

SID
(Under his breath.)
Pretty thin, as long a dream as that without any mistakes in it.

(Actors freeze briefly. MARK TWAIN enters. Actors begin setting the school scene.)

MARK TWAIN
Now that Tom was covered in glory, he was quite sure Becky Thatcher would fall all over herself to make up. Yet for all his worldly wisdom, it is clear that Tom Sawyer knew very little about women. We should not fault him too far, however, as many of us who have lived a considerable time longer know very little more about the fair sex and than Tom did.

Becky, being feminine to the core, not only refused to make up, but had concocted to establish a bosom friendship with Amy

Lawrence, and the two contrived together to make Tom's life miserable. As always the weaker sex gives in first...and so it was that Tom decided to apologize.

> (MARK TWAIN exits. The children are in their seats. MR. WALTERS is at his desk reading a thick book.)

BECKY
Say, I wonder what's in that book that Mr. Walters is always readin'?

AMY
I'd give a heap to find out. But he always keeps it locked up in his desk when he ain't reading it.

MR. WALTERS
Lunch time, children. I have an errand I must attend to, but I shall return before lessons commence this afternoon.

> (All the children except for BECKY and AMY leave, as does MR. WALTERS, who fails to lock up his book. BECKY and AMY prepare to eat their lunch together in the school room.)

AMY
Looky yonder. Mr. Walters left his book out on his desk. I don't ever remember him doing that before.

BECKY
No, indeed. Why do you suppose he did that?

AMY
Perhaps he don't care if someone looks in it no more.

BECKY

Do you really thinks so? Perhaps it wouldn't hurt if we just have a quick peek. I'm dyin' to know what's in it.

(TOM enters, but doesn't see AMY.)

TOM

I been acting awful lately, Becky, and I'm sorry. I won't ever act that way again, as long as I live. Please make up, won't you?

AMY

My, my. It sounds like a voice from beyond the grave. I understand promise-breakers are doomed to walk the earth, seeking forgiveness from those they wronged, but they never get it, so they have to just keep roaming forever and ever.

(TOM suddenly realizes his predicament, but it's too late, so he presses forward.)

TOM

Please, Becky. I...

BECKY

I'll thank you to keep yourself to yourself, Mr. Thomas Sawyer. I'll never speak to you again.

TOM

Well, who cares, Miss Smarty?

(TOM exits.)

AMY

Good riddance! I'm going to tell everyone I see how Tom Sawyer came crawling back trying to make up to you, and how you turned him down. That'll show him.

(AMY exits. BECKY tries to eat her lunch but finds no pleasure in it. Her anger at TOM is overcome by her curiosity at MR. WALTERS' book. Pretending to stroll around the room, she makes sure she is quite alone, and then sneaks up to MR. WALTERS' desk and opens the book. At that moment, TOM walks back in.)

TOM

Becky, I gotta…

(Startled, BECKY rips the page she is looking at.)

BECKY

Tom Sawyer, you are just as mean as you can be, to sneak up on a person and look at what they're looking at.

TOM

How could I know you was looking at anything?

BECKY

You're going to tell on me, and I'll be whipped. I never was whipped in school before. How you can be so mean?

(TOM is stunned speechless, and now the other children are beginning to gather, and MR. WALTERS enters. There is nothing left to do but sit down and await the inevitable. MR. WALTERS immediately sees his book has been tampered with, opens it and finds the torn page. He is furious.)

MR. WALTERS

Who tore this book? Benjamin Rogers, did you tear this book?

BEN
No, sir!

MR. WALTERS
Joseph Harper, did you?

JOE
Warn't me, Mr. Walters

MR. WALTERS
Amy Lawrence?

AMY
No, sir.

MR. WALTERS
Rebecca Thatcher. did you tear - no, look me in the face. Did you tear this book?

TOM
I done it!

MR. WALTERS
What!?

TOM
I tore your book, Mr. Walters. I'm awful sorry.

MR. WALTERS
You will be sorrier still. Come here!

> (TOM approaches the seat of judgment as MR.
> WALTERS reaches for the paddle. TOM bends
> over and puts his hands on MR. WALTERS'
> desk. MR. WALTERS raises the paddle, then all
> actors freeze momentarily. MARK TWAIN

enters. As TWAIN begins to speak, the actors
exit.)

MARK TWAIN
The children stared in perplexity at this incredible folly. Tom
stood a moment, to gather his dismembered faculties; and when
he stepped forward to go to his punishment, the surprise, the
gratitude, the adoration that shone upon him out of Becky's eyes
seemed pay enough for a hundred floggings. Inspired by the
splendor of his own act, he took without an outcry the most
merciless flaying that Mr. Walters had ever administered; and
received with indifference the added cruelty of a command to
remain two hours after school, for he knew who would wait for
him outside till his captivity was done.

However, when Tom arrived at home his euphoria crumbled into
dismay.

(MARK TWAIN exits. Lights rise on AUNT
POLLY'S home.)

AUNT POLLY
Tom, I've a notion to skin you alive!

TOM
Aint Polly, what have I done?

AUNT POLLY
Well, you've done enough, I reckon. Here I go over to Sereny
Harper, expecting I'm going to make her believe all that rubbage
about that dream, when lo and behold she'd found out from Joe
that you was over here and heard all the talk we had that night.
Tom, it makes me feel so bad to think you could let me go and
make such a fool of myself and never say a word.

TOM

I wish I hadn't done it, but I didn't think.

AUNT POLLY

Oh, child, you never think of anything but your own self. You could think to come all the way over here from Jackson's Island in the night to laugh at our troubles, and you could think to fool me with a lie about a dream; but you couldn't ever think to pity us and save us from sorrow.

TOM

Aint Polly, I know now it was mean, but I didn't mean to be mean. Honest. And besides, I didn't come over here to laugh at you that night. It was to tell you not to be uneasy about us, because we hadn't got drownded.

AUNT POLLY

Oh, Tom, don't lie. It only makes things a hundred times worse.

TOM

It ain't a lie, Aint Polly; it's the truth. I wanted to keep you from grieving. That was all that made me come.

AUNT POLLY

I'd give the whole world to believe that. It would cover up a power of sins, Tom. But it ain't reasonable. Why didn't you tell me, child?

TOM

Why, you see, when you got to talking about the funeral, I just got all full of the idea of our coming and hiding in the church, and I couldn't bear to spoil it. So I just put the letter back in my pocket and kept mum.

AUNT POLLY

What letter?

TOM

The letter I wrote to tell you we'd gone piratin'. I wish, now, I'd a' left it. I do, honest.

AUNT POLLY

Well, it might be the truth it and might not. Be off with you now, and don't bother me any more.

> (TOM exits. AUNT POLLY picks up TOM'S jacket and starts to go through his pockets.)

I reckon he's lied about it, but it's a blessed lie. There's such a comfort come from it. I know the Lord will forgive him. But I don't want to find out it's a lie. I won't look.

> (Finally, curiosity gets the better of her, she reaches into the pocket and finds the letter.)

I could forgive the boy, now, if he'd committed a million sins!

(BLACKOUT. END OF ACT II)

ACT III

SETTING: AUNT POLLY'S home.

AT RISE: Actors begin setting the stage with the church on one side, and AUNT POLLY'S home on the other. HUCKLEBERRY FINN rushes forward.

HUCK
This here's the most excitin' part of the whole story. See, me and Tom knew that Injun Joe and that other feller hid a bunch o' gold some'ers, and we was determined to find it. Little did we know that...

(MARK TWAIN enters.)

MARK TWAIN
Some "where's" Huckleberry; not "some'ers." Now, talking with the audience is my job. And I believe yours is *some'ers* back there?

(HUCK nods and exits.)

MARK TWAIN
The end of school may be the most exciting time in any child's year. Yes, there were summer chores, but there was also plenty of time for playing "hispy" and "gully-keeper" a dozen other games you folks nowadays have no recollection of. But the event of greatest anticipation was the village's annual picnic at

McDougal's cave.

The grounds were three miles below town and required a ferryboat ride to get there. There were games and explorations and massive quantities of food followed by a season of rest and chat in the shade of spreading oaks. Finally somebody shouted, "Who's ready for the cave?"

Everybody was. Bundles of candles were procured, and straightway there was a general procession that went filing down the steep descent of the main avenue, the flickering candlelight dimly revealing the lofty rock walls that extended almost sixty feet overhead. One might wander days and nights together through its intricate tangle of rifts and chasms, and never find its end – for no man really "knew" the cave.

By-and-by, adventurers came straggling back to the mouth of the cave, laughing, panting, smeared from head to foot with tallow drippings, daubed with clay and entirely delighted with the success of the day. Meanwhile, back in town, there was other, less honorable business, afoot.

> (HUCK rushes up to AUNT POLLY'S house banging on the door.)

HUCK
Miss Polly, Miss Polly! Open the door, quick!

AUNT POLLY
What's the row there? Who's banging? What do you want?

HUCK
It's Huckleberry Finn, Miss Polly. Please let me in!

AUNT POLLY
Huckleberry Finn, indeed! It ain't a name to open many doors, I

judge. But you're always welcome at this house.

> (AUNT POLLY opens the door, and HUCK rushes in.)

Now, what's the trouble.

HUCK

Please don't never tell I told you. Please don't. I'd be killed, sure.

AUNT POLLY

Land sakes, child, out with it. I won't tell if you don't want me to. What troubles you so?

HUCK

I was all balled up trying to sleep down by the Temperance Tavern, when along comes these two fellers slipping along close by me, with something under their arm, and I reckoned they'd stole it. One was a-smoking, and t'other wanted a light; so they stopped right before me and the cigars lit up their faces and I see that the big one was that deaf and dumb Spaniard that's been hanging around town. T'other one was a rusty, ragged-looking devil.

AUNT POLLY

Slow down, Huckleberry. Mary! Mary! Fetch Huckleberry some water.

> (MARY and SID enter. MARY fetches the water while SID listens.)

What happened then?

HUCK

I follered 'em. I wanted to see what they was up to, sneakin' around like that. I dogged 'em to the widder Douglas's back fence, and stood in the dark and heard the Spaniard swear he'd spile the widder's looks. He said, the widder's husband was rough on him when he was Justice of the Peace, and had him jailed for a vagrant, and horsewhipped too. He said since Mr. Douglas was dead he was going to take his revenge on his Widder. He said he was going to slit her nostrils and notch her ears like a sow.

AUNT POLLY
Bosch, Huckleberry. That Spaniard ain't been around town for more'n a couple of weeks, and Mr. Douglas has been dead these past five years. And how'd he talk if he was deaf and dumb?

HUCK
Oh, Miss Polly. 'Tain't a Spaniard at all. It's Injun Joe! I was awful scared and I lit a shuck and didn't stop till I got here.

AUNT POLLY
Sid, you run quick now, and fetch the sheriff.

(SID exits. AUNT POLLY gives HUCK a hug.)

AUNT POLLY
Poor lad, you look as if you'd had a hard night of it. Why, Huckleberry, you're burning up. You ain't well a bit. No wonder you're flighty and off your balance.

(MARY and AUNT POLLY get HUCK into TOM'S bed. HUCK is rapidly becoming delirious.)

HUCK
Miss Polly, where's Tom? I gotta warn Tom. Injun Joe is back.

AUNT POLLY
He ain't come home from the picnic yet. Like as not he's spending the night at Joe Harper's. You just sleep now, and don't you worry. The sheriff'll take care of Injun Joe.

(Lights fade. On rise, the congregation is assembling at the church.)

WIDOW DOUGLAS

Polly, I can't thank you enough. I cannot imagine what might have happened if not for you.

AUNT POLLY

Don't say a word about it, Sarah. There's another that you're more beholden to I. But he don't allow me to tell his name. The sheriff and his men wouldn't have been there but for him.

MRS. THATCHER

Horrible. Simply horrible. I understand one of those men was found drowned in the river, but that Injun Joe managed to escape. Don't you fret, Sarah. They'll catch him.

(AMY LAWRENCE walks by.)

MRS. THATCHER

Well, Amy. I wondered if you children were going to sleep all day. Of course I just expected you all would be tired to death. Uh, where's Becky?

AMY

Becky? I'm sorry, Mrs. Thatcher. I don't know what you are talking about.

MRS. THATCHER

Didn't she stay with you last night?

AMY

Why, no, ma'am. Was she supposed to?

MRS. THATCHER

It was so late when everyone came home...I just assumed...

AUNT POLLY

Sereny, I've got a boy that's turned up missing. I reckon my Tom stayed at your house last night, and now he's afraid to come to church. I've got to settle with him.

MRS. HARPER

He didn't stay with us, Polly. Joe, have you seen Tom today?

JOE

No'm.

AUNT POLLY

When did you see him last?

JOE

I can't rightly remember, not that I could say for sure. I remember him going into the cave holdin' hands with Becky. I don't 'member seeing him after that.

AMY

And I don't remember seeing either of them on the ferry boat on the way home. I was going to ask Becky to come to my birthday party next month, but I couldn't find her.

AUNT POLLY

Merciful lord in heaven. You don't think they're still in the cave?

> (Blackout. All that is visible now is a pair of candles, held by TOM and BECKY. They roam slowly, aimlessly around the stage. They are lost in the cave.)

BECKY

I didn't notice, but it seems ever so long since I heard any of the others. I wonder how long we've been down here?

TOM

Long enough, I reckon.

BECKY

Can you find the way? It's all a mixed-up crookedness to me.

TOM

I don't know. When those bats chased us I kind of lost track.

BECKY

I hope we won't get lost. It would be so awful.

TOM

I don't think this is the right way. No, this ain't the one, but we'll come to it directly.

BECKY

Oh, Tom, We seem to get worse and worse off all the time.

TOM

Listen.

> (Silence. TOM shouts, and his voice echoes in the darkness.)

Hello! Hello! Anybody there?

BECKY

Oh, don't yell again, Tom, it is too horrid.

TOM

It is horrid, but I better, Becky; somebody might hear us.

BECKY

Might? Tom, you think we're really lost? Oh, why did we ever leave the others!

> (TOM takes BECKY'S candle and blows it out.)

TOM

We might need this for later. Now don't fret, Becky. We'll get out of this.

BECKY

Tom, I am so hungry.

TOM

I've got a bit of cheese left from the picnic. I wish it was as big as a barrel, for it's all we've got. I think we better stay here. There's a little spring, so we'll have water to drink.

BECKY

Tom, they'll miss us and hunt for us. Won't they?

TOM

Yes, they will. Of course they will!

BECKY

Maybe they're hunting for us now, Tom. They would miss us when we didn't get back on the boat.

TOM

I reckon they would. I hope they would.

> (The candle sputters out, and it is totally dark. Lights rise on AUNT POLLY'S home. AUNT POLLY, MRS. THATCHER, MRS. HARPER and MARY are all awaiting word. HUCK is in bed, delirious with fever. The WIDOW DOUGLAS arrives.)

WIDOW DOUGLAS

Any word, Polly?

AUNT POLLY

The men have been searching all night. This morning they sent a message by my Sid. 'Send more candles. Send food.' Nothing more.

WIDOW DOUGLAS

They'll be found. Trust the Good Lord. And how is your young Huckleberry Finn?

AUNT POLLY

Burning up with the fever. I mean to do my best by him, because whether he's good, bad or indifferent, he is the Lord's, and nothing that is the Lord's is a thing to be neglected. Huckleberry has good spots in him, though they are a might hard to see.

WIDOW DOUGLAS

You can depend on it. That's the Lord's mark. He don't leave it off. He puts it somewhere on every creature that comes from his hands. Poor boy.

> (JEFF THATCHER enters. He is covered in mud and candle soot, and bordering on exhaustion.)

JEFF THATCHER

We've ransacked portions of that cavern that have never been visited before; every corner, every crevice. In one place, far from where everyone usually goes, they found the names "BECKY & TOM" traced upon the wall with candle-smoke, and near at hand…this.

> (He holds out a grease-soiled bit of ribbon. MRS. THATCHER recognizes it as BECKY'S.)

MRS. THATCHER

Becky's hair ribbon. She's lost. She's never coming home.

JEFF THATCHER

We're not giving up, but we must go in shifts, now. I got to rest for a few moments, and then I'll return.

> (Lights fade to black. We are back in the cave. TOM strikes a match and lights his last candle. There is a flicker of a candle off to the side.)

TOM

Becky. Becky! I see a light. It's a candle, Becky! We're found! Hey! Over here! We're over here!

> (The candle starts to recede.)

I don't think they heard me. Here, hold on to this kite string, so I can find my way back. I'm gonna chase them down.

> (TOM works his way through the darkness toward the candle, yelling all the while. With one final shout he comes close to the candle, and comes face to face with INJUN JOE. Both let out a startled shout and run off in opposite directions. TOM stops to catch his breath when he notices a speck of light.)

TOM

Becky. Becky! I found a way out! Follow the string, Becky!

> (Lights fade in the cave. Lights up on AUNT POLLY'S home. MR. WALTERS, shouting all the way, runs up to the door and starts banging.)

MR. WALTERS

Turn out! Turn out! They're found! They're found!

> (AUNT POLLY and MRS. THATCHER come outside in time to see JUDGE THATCHER carrying BECKY with TOM walking by his side. They rush to embrace them, then usher

them inside. Once TOM and BECKY are resting
on the sofa, the story unfolds.)

TOM
Becky was too tired to go any further, so I left her by the spring
and went on an exploring expedition. I followed two passages as
far as my kite string would reach, and explored down a third
passage, and I was just about to turn back when I glimpsed a far-
off speck that looked like daylight. I dropped the string and
groped toward it, and pushed my head and shoulders through a
little hole, and there was the river rolling by!

If it had only happened to be night I would have missed that
speck of daylight and would not have explored that passage any
more.

JUDGE THATCHER
Some men came along in a skiff and Tom hailed them and told
them their situation. The men didn't believe their wild tale at
first, because they were five miles down the river below the
valley the cave is in. They took them aboard, rowed to a house,
gave them supper, made them rest a few hours and then brought
them home.

(Lights fade to black. Spot on MARK TWAIN.)

MARK TWAIN
Three days and nights of toil and hunger in the cave were not to
be shaken off at once, as Tom and Becky soon discovered. They
were bed-ridden all of Wednesday and Thursday. Tom got out a
little on Thursday and was nearly as whole as ever by Saturday;
but Becky did not leave her room until Sunday, and even then
she looked as if she had passed through a wasting illness.

The Widow Douglas had taken over the care of Huckleberry
Finn, saying Aunt Polly could not be expected to care for two

invalids at the same time. Tom went to see Huck on Friday, but was warned to keep still about his adventure and introduce no exciting topic. The Widow Douglas stayed by to see that he obeyed.

About a fortnight later, while on his way to visit Huck, Tom happened meet Judge Thatcher and his brother, Jeff.

(Lights rise.)

JEFF THATCHER
So, Tom. How would you like to take another adventure into the cave.

TOM
I reckon I wouldn't mind it.

JUDGE THATCHER
Well, there are plenty of others just like you, Tom, I've not the least doubt. But we have taken care of that. Nobody will get lost in that cave any more.

TOM
Why's that, Judge?

JUDGE THATCHER
Because I had its big door sheathed with boiler iron two weeks ago, and triple-locked. And I've got the keys.

JEFF THATCHER
What's the matter, boy? Are you all right? You look like you've seen a ghost.

TOM
Oh, Judge, Injun Joe's in the cave.

(Actors freeze momentarily, then exit. MARK TWAIN remains.)

MARK TWAIN
Within a few minutes the news had spread, and a dozen skiff-loads of men were on their way to McDougal's cave. When the cave door was unlocked, Injun Joe lay stretched upon the ground, dead, with his face close to the crack of the door, as if his longing eyes had been fixed, to the last moment, upon the light and the cheer of the free world outside.

He was buried near the mouth of the cave; and people flocked there in boats and wagons from all the farms and hamlets for seven miles around. They brought their children, and all sorts of provisions, and confessed that they had almost as satisfactory a time at the funeral as they could have had at the hanging.

The next morning Tom took Huck to a private place to have an important talk.

TOM
Huck, I know where the money is. It's in the cave!

HUCK
Tom, you wouldn't fun a feller would you? You in earnest?

TOM
Earnest, Huck. Just as earnest as ever I was in my life. Will you go in there with me and help get it out?

HUCK
You bet I will! I will if it's where we can blaze our way to it and not get lost. But Judge Thatcher's done bolted the door agin. How we gonna get in?

TOM

The same way I got out!

HUCK

Good as wheat! When do we go for it?

TOM

Right now. We'll be rich, Huck. And that cave will make a dandy hideout. We'll get Joe Harper, and turn robbers, and be Tom Sawyer's gang.

>   (TOM and HUCK spit on their hands and shake.
>   Lights fade to black. When they rise again,
>   TOM and HUCK are pulling a wagon that is
>   obviously heavy. It's contents are covered by a
>   cloth.)

SID

Tom. Tom! I been lookin' ever'where for you. Aint Polly says for you to come home quick. And she said to bring Huckleberry with you, 'cause like as not you was together.

TOM

What's it all about, Sid?

SID

Aint Polly said you'll see when the Widder Douglas gets there. But she's already there, so y'all got to light a shuck.

HUCK

What have we done?

TOM

Nuthin' I can think of.

>   (When the boys arrive at AUNT POLLY'S

home they discover a large gathering waiting on
them.)

SID
I found 'em, Aint Polly. I brought 'em home just like you said.

AUNT POLLY
And you did just right. Come inside, boys. There's some folks
wants to talk to you.

WIDOW DOUGLAS
Home the conquering heroes.

JUDGE THATCHER
Sit down, boys. And quit your fidgeting as if you've done
something wrong. We not here to pin your ears back. As a matter
of fact, we are all quite proud of these two fine citizens, and
believe it's high time this town showed it. Tom, because of the
uncommon bravery you've shown on more than one occasion,
I've decided to take you on as my apprentice. And I believe Mrs.
Douglas has something she would like to say.

WIDOW DOUGLAS
It does not take someone with a passel of book learning to figure
out who it was that kept two scoundrels from doing me serious
harm. I mean to pay my debt. Huckleberry Finn – I mean to give
you a home under my roof and give you a proper education. And
when I can spare the money I intend to start you up in business
in a modest way.

TOM
Shucks, Widder. Huck don't need it. Huck's rich. He's got lots
of money. Oh, you needn't smile. I reckon I can show you. You
just wait a minute.

(TOM runs out the door and grabs the bags

(TOM entered, struggling with the weight of his
sacks, and pours the mass of yellow coin upon
the table.)

    hidden in the wagon.)

AUNT POLLY

Sid, what ails Tom? He...well, there ain't ever any making of
that boy out. I never...

(TOM entered, struggling with the weight of his
sacks, and pours the mass of yellow coin upon
the table.)

TOM

There. What did I tell you? Half of it's Huck's and half of it's
mine!

JUDGE THATCHER

Well, I thought I had fixed up a little surprise for this occasion,
but it don't amount to anything now.

(All actors freeze momentarily, then begin to
clear the stage back to it's bare condition. Only
the whitewashed fence remains. All actors exit,
except HUCK, who sits in front of the fence.
MARK TWAIN enters.)

MARK TWAIN

The money amounted to a little over twelve thousand dollars -
more than any one present had ever seen at one time before. So
vast a sum, all in actual cash, seemed next to incredible. It was
talked about, gloated over, glorified, until the reason of many of
the citizens tottered under the strain of unhealthy excitement.

The Widow Douglas put Huck's money out at six per cent, and
Judge Thatcher did the same with Tom's. Each lad had an
income, now, that was simply prodigious - a dollar for every
week-day in the year and half of the Sundays. It was just what
the minister got. No, it was what he was promised, but generally

couldn't collect.

Huck Finn's wealth and the fact that he was now under the Widow Douglas' protection introduced him into society – or rather, dragged him into it. And his sufferings were almost more than he could bear. He bravely bore his miseries for three weeks, and then one day turned up missing.

(MARK TWAIN exits as TOM enters.)

HUCK
Don't talk about it, Tom. I've tried it, and it ain't for me. The widder's good to me, and friendly; but I cain't stand her ways. She makes me get up just at the same time every morning; she makes me wash, she combs me all to thunder; she won't let me sleep in the woodshed; I got to wear them blamed clothes that just smother me, Tom; and they're so rotten nice that I can't set down, nor lay down, nor roll around anywhere's. I got to go to church, I cain't ketch a fly in there, and I cain't chaw, and I got to wear shoes all day on Sunday. The widder eats by a bell. She goes to bed by a bell. She gits up by a bell. Everything's so awful reg'lar a body cain't stand it.

TOM
Well, everybody does that way, Huck.

HUCK
I ain't everybody, and I cain't stand it. I got to ask to go a-fishing; I got to ask to go in a-swimming. Dern'd if I hain't got to ask to do everything. And I got to talk so nice all the time. I had to go up in the attic and cuss for awhile just to git the taste back in my mouth. The widder, she won't let me smoke; she won't let me yell, she won't let me gape, nor stretch, nor scratch. And dad-fetch it, she prays all the time! I had to shove off, Tom. I just had to.

Looky-here, Tom, being rich ain't what it's cracked up to be. It's just worry and sweat, and sweat and worry, and a-wishing you was dead all the time. I wouldn't ever got into all this trouble if it hadn't been for that money. Now you just take my share of it along with your'n, and you go and beg off for me with the widder.

TOM

Oh, Huck, you know I can't do that. 'Tain't fair; and besides, if you'll try this thing just a while longer you'll come to like it.

HUCK

Oh, yes, the way I'd like sittin' on a hot stove if I was to sit on it long enough. No, Tom, I won't be rich, and I won't live in them cussed smothery houses. Blame it all! Just as we'd got a cave, and was all just fixed to be robbers, here this dern foolishness has got to come up and spile it all.

TOM

Looky-here, Huck, being rich ain't going to keep me back from turning robber.

HUCK

No? Oh, good-licks; are you in real dead-wood earnest, Tom?

TOM

Just as dead earnest as I'm sitting here. But Huck, we can't let you into the gang if you ain't respectable.

HUCK

Cain't let me in, Tom? Didn't you let me go for a pirate?

TOM

Yes, but that's different. A robber is more high-toned than what a pirate is, as a general rule. In most countries they're awful high up in the nobility - dukes and such.

HUCK

Now, Tom, we always been friends, ain't we? You wouldn't shet me out, now, would you, Tom?

TOM

Huck, I wouldn't want to, but what would people say? Why, they'd say, 'Mph! Tom Sawyer's Gang! Pretty low characters in it!' They'd mean you, Huck. You wouldn't like that, and I wouldn't.

HUCK

Well, I'll go back to the widder for a month and tackle it and see if I can come to stand it, if you'll let me belong to the gang, Tom.

TOM

All right, Huck, it's a deal! Come along, and I'll ask the widow to let up on you a little.

HUCK

Will you, Tom? Will you really? That's good. If she'll let up on some of the roughest things, I'll smoke private and cuss private. When you going to start the gang?

TOM

Oh, right off. Here comes Joe Harper now. We'll have the initiation to-night and swear to stand by one another, and never tell the gang's secrets, even if you're chopped all to flinders.

> (JOE HARPER enters. The three boys freeze as
> MARK TWAIN enters. Lights fade slowly, until
> only the boys are bathed in the spot light.)

MARK TWAIN

When one writes a story about grown people, he knows exactly where to stop, that is, with a marriage. But when he writes of juveniles, he must stop where he best can. This story could not go much further without becoming the history of a man, and since this is strictly a history of a boy, here is where Tom's story must stop.

Of course the tale does not end here. Each of the boys went on to great tussles and greater glory. Why I could spend hours telling you about Huckleberry Finn's wild adventures floating down the mighty Mississippi on a raft...but that's another story.

BLACKOUT

Made in the USA
Lexington, KY
30 July 2019